IMAGES BY DESIC

THE PHOTOGRAPHY OF

DAVID HERROD

CREATIVE MONOCHROME
CONTEMPORARY PORTFOLIO SERIES

DAVID HERROD is a prolific and versatile photographer whose work has been published in several books, newspapers and magazines. His images have been successful in many competitions and his numerous exhibition acceptances and awards have gained him the prized distinction of Artist of the International Federation of Photographic Art.

David is best known for his exquisite landscape photography, particularly of the Lake District, as featured in his major publication for Creative Monochrome, *The Waters of Cumbria*. But he is equally at home with architectural, commercial, fashion and portrait photography, using the medium to portray beauty in all its forms.

IMAGES BY DESIGN
The photography of
DAVID HERROD

Published in the UK by Creative Monochrome Ltd
20 St Peters Road, Croydon, Surrey, CR0 1HD.
© Creative Monochrome Ltd, 1995.

British Library Cataloguing-in-Publication Data:
A catalogue record for this book is available from
the British Library

ISBN 1 873319 18 5
First edition, 1995

Printed in England by Butler & Tanner Ltd,
Caxton Road, Frome, Somerset.

INTRODUCTION
DAVID HERROD

It was at about the age of 14 that the interest in photography really took hold of me. A trade with a school friend gave me the ownership of a kit of photographic chemicals, paper, a contact printing frame and negatives of film stars of the time. I had no camera, but this simple kit was enough to reveal the magic of printing a photograph – an experience from which I have never 'recovered'.

When I think back, it was really a miracle. Not the process itself, but the fact that, under the appalling conditions in which it was carried out, any positive image was ever obtained.

The darkroom was an outhouse with light leaking in around the door. The processing dishes were rusty old baking trays. Exposure was made by switching on an electric bulb and guessing the time required. There was no safelight, but enough daylight leaked in to enable a friend and me to see what was happening and to experience the thrill of seeing an image appear on the paper in the murky developer solution. Discoloured and fogged it was, but we knew nothing about print quality. The fact that we had produced an image was electrifying.

I can remember the tingle of excitement very easily because I still get it, every time I print.

That was my baptism into photography. For quite a few years after that, I pursued photography still without a camera of my own – making photographs by begging and borrowing cameras from members of my family.

Photography, eventually with my own camera, became my hobby. Not my only hobby, but one of my most important ones. To pursue it as a career did not, regrettably, occur to me until many years later, and I am thankful that I now have the opportunity – better late than never.

For my early career, I turned to the building and civil engineering industry and became a Chartered Civil Engineer. At first, I worked in close conjunction with architects, but then moved more into pure civil engineering. Design – under one of the several dictionary definitions of the term: "to work out the structure or form of something, as by making a sketch, outline, pattern or plan" – was now my bread and butter.

Carving out this career took up most of my time and energy, and consequently my photography stagnated. Fortunately, it did not die. As the pressure from my career eased, the suppressed desire to make photographs grew and became more productive. My images seemed to be appreciated by others, which gave me great encouragement. I became quite prolific.

Looking back, I think the reason was that my main career had changed. Whereas it had started as a creative one, where I was directly producing something, it had become a managerial role, where I was more remote from the 'action'. Balancing this change, my creative urge was satisfied by making photographs – photographs that people wanted to buy. When the opportunity came for me to leave behind my engineering career, it was an easy transition to move into photography in a more serious way.

Although my output now is influenced by commercial demands, I am still able to indulge in my own delights. I photograph all manner of subjects and some of these – and my treatment of them – reflect my early training.

The title of this collection of photographs was not chosen by me. I find it very revealing to hear the views of others about my work – sometimes they pinpoint things which are so obvious that they had passed me by.

Some of my work, I am told, has a strong design feel to it. In this case, though, in another definition of the word: "a coherent or purposeful pattern, as opposed to chaos". If this does fit, then I can take no credit for it. The elements of any design I happen to photograph have been arranged by other forces, not by me. I only see them.

This is the spin-off which makes photography such a joy for me. It develops in me a keener perception of things around me. Many people seem to be blinkered: only the garish, or shocking, objects seem to attract their attention. A fact that advertisers and retailers exploit. One piece of advice I give to those who attend my lectures and workshops is to practice 'a roving eye'. Next time you walk down the High Street, don't look at the shop windows, but look at the buildings above them – I guarantee that you will see things you had never been aware of. Then having expanded your vision, allow your emotions some freedom. Do not supress them: react to them and let them dictate what you photograph.

I feel that many people who indulge in photography treat it as a technical exercise. They become as obsessed by this aspect as those 'buffs' for whom sound reproduction has become such a search for perfection that they no longer listen to the music, but instead listen for flaws. The real objective has been lost.

Look and see. Designs are everywhere. Mathematicians will tell you that even in chaos there are designs.

PORTFOLIO

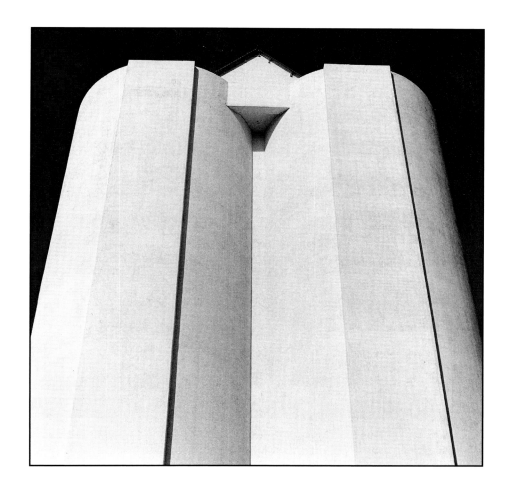

#1

#2

#3

#4

#5

#6

#7

#8

#9

#10 *(top)*, **#11** *(below)*

#12 *(top)*, **#13** *(below)*

#14

#15 *(top)*, **#16** *(below)*

#17

#18

#19

#20

#21 *(top)*, *#22* *(below)*

#23 (top), #24 (below)

23

#25

#26

#27

#28

#29

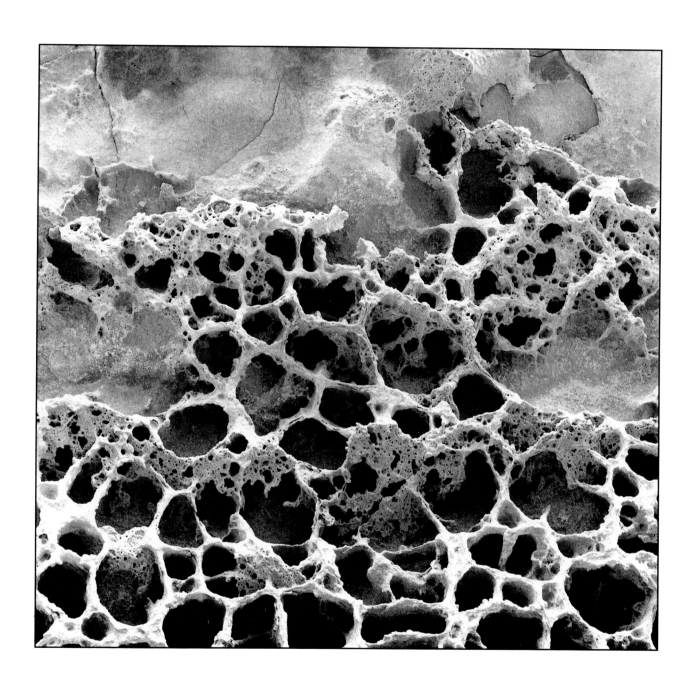

#30

#31

#32

#33

#34

#35

#36

#37

#38

#39

#40

#41

#42

#43

#44

#45

#46

#47

#48

#49

For further details of the Contemporary Portfolio Series
and a catalogue of Creative Monochrome publications,
please write to Creative Monochrome Limited,
20 St Peters Road, Croydon, Surrey, CR0 1HD, England.